I0224408

7 Success Secrets That Every College Student Needs to Know!

7 Success Secrets That Every College Student
Needs to Know!
By Alfred Poor

Copyright © 2012 by Alfred Poor

All rights reserved. No portion of this book may be reproduced mechanically, electronically, or by any other means, including photocopying, without written permission of the publisher. It is illegal to copy this book, post it to a website, or distribute it by any other means without permission from the publisher.

September 2012

ISBN 978-0- 9826526-7-1

Published by:
Desktop Wings Inc.
700 East Walnut Street
Perkasie, PA 18944
215-453-9312
www.desktopwings.com

7 Success Secrets That Every College Student Needs to Know!

Strategies to Get a Job, Keep It, and Speed That Next Promotion

Alfred Poor

Acknowledgements

Once again, my family and friends have patiently endured the development of another book. I have spent the past year or more, bending their ears as I worked out the concepts that I present here. As always, many of the best points that you find in these pages were made better by the contributions of others, while I take sole responsibility for any weaknesses.

I specifically want to thank two people who I count among my friends and colleagues. John Formica and Ken Davis are excellent speakers and authors, and I appreciate the help they gave me in previewing the manuscript.

I also want to thank Felicia Slattery for her help and support, not only with this book but also in shaping my entire college and corporate speaking programs based on my "7 Success Secrets."

I also tip my fedora (or two) to my friend and mentor, Joe King. He has been a valued sounding board throughout, and is my accountability buddy who holds me to the promises I make to myself and to him.

My daughter Anna and my wife Bebe deserve the major share of the credit for this project. In addition to providing keen eyes for catching the errors in this text, they also have challenged me with probing questions and gifted me with valuable insights and suggestions that have made this book much better than it was when I first started.

Dedication

I dedicate this book to all the people who have taken the time
to try to share their knowledge with me. To all my teachers
and professors, all my bosses and work colleagues, to all the
writers and speakers, to all my friends and acquaintances, and
most of all to my family, I thank you for helping me learn the
lessons that have brought so much happiness and success in
my life. I am a fortunate man indeed.

Watch your thoughts,
> for they become words.

Watch your words,
> for they become actions.

Watch your actions,
> for they become habits.

Watch your habits,
> for they become character.

Watch your character,
> for it becomes your destiny.

Anonymous[1]

---

[1] This quote is widely attributed to the Chinese philosopher Lao Tzu, but I have been unable to find a definitive reference that identifies him as the source.

Foreword

This book is **AWESOME!** Not only does it have important information, but I really enjoyed reading it. "7 Success Secrets That Every College Student Needs to Know" is packed with great ideas and principles. It not only will be a help to college students, but I know a whole bunch of employees of businesses that need to read this as well.

As America's Customer Experience Coach, I get to work with businesses and organizations throughout the U.S. and help them transform their current service level into a magical customer experience. "7 Success Secrets" gives college students the key ingredients that they need to create their own magical career experience. I believe that it should be a must read on any college campus.

Alfred shares his incredible knowledge and street-smart wisdom in an easy to read book that is so crammed with powerful tips that it is sure to be a lifetime valuable resource.

I have no doubt that Alfred has become a college student's most valuable resource in charting a path to success in that important first job after graduation. He clearly respects and cares about his audience, and wants to help them find fulfillment and satisfaction in their work.

I'm happy to say that my own two sons will be the first to get copies, and I am definitely recommending this book to all my clients and their employees.

John Formica, America's Customer Experience Coach and author of *Making the Customer Experience Magical Now! How to Succeed in Business and Beat Out Your Competition Today!*

Table of Contents

Foreword viii

Introduction 1

   Internships Are Not Always the Answer...............................2

   Hit the Ground Running 3

Success Secret #1: Everyone Is a Customer 5

   Lessons from Fast Food...5

   A Great Place to Work...7

   The Cost of Negativity..9

   Who Do You Work For?..9

   The Customer Experience...11

   The Big Question...13

   What Goes Around 14

   Success Secret #1 Action Guide...16

Success Secret #2: Make Everyone's Job Easier....................18

   Thoughtful Acts 19

   Visible Dividends 20

   Taking Care of Typos..20

   A Little Thought 22

   Don't Hand Off Trouble...23

   The Golden Rule in Disguise 25

   Success Secret #2 Action Guide...26

Success Secret #3: Dress for Success 28

    Instinctive Behaviors.. 28

    People Are Animals Too.. 29

    Context Counts.. 31

    Aim High 32

    Accelerate Your Progress... 33

    But Not Too High... 34

    When You Have No Choice.. 35

    Make a Statement 36

    Success Secret #3 Action Guide... 38

Success Secret #4: Over-Deliver on Your Promises............. 40

    A Tale from the Dark Ages 40

    What Happened Here? 42

    Consider the Alternative.. 43

    No Need for Super Powers 43

    What Is at Work Here?... 45

    Success Secret #4 Action Guide... 47

Success Secret #5: Communicate Early and Often............. 49

    The Box in the Driveway 50

    Communication Choices.. 51

    When Bad Things Happen to Good Plans.......................... 53

    Take the Long View... 54

    Pick the Right Person 55

    Take Action Early... 57

Success Secret #5 Action Guide.............................59

Success Secret #6: Be Flexible..............................61

    Plenty of Stress...61

    Be the Bamboo...63

    Nobody Home?...64

    Matchmaker 66

    Impossible Deadlines 67

    Take Note...69

    Interpersonal Stress 71

    Don't Take It Personally...............................72

    Learn to Bend...73

    Success Secret #6 Action Guide.....................74

Success Secret #7: Always Be Marketing..............76

    Someone Is Listening...................................77

    Hot Summers..78

    What Will You Say? 79

    Don't Say It...81

    It's Also about You.......................................82

    Help Your Company 83

    Success Secret #7 Action Guide.....................86

Put the Seven Secrets to Work for Your Success!.....88

    Put the Success Secrets to Work Action Guide 91

About the Author...94

Introduction

When I graduated from college, the job market was difficult, especially in my chosen field of education. But that was nothing compared to the situation facing the typical college graduate these days. High unemployment rates make it difficult for students to find jobs of any sort, let alone one in an area for which they have prepared.

According to a Rutgers study of students who have graduated from a four year college program within the past five years, only 51% currently have a full time job. Many of the remainder report that they have two or more part time jobs, or no job at all. And of those with full time jobs, fewer than two out of five reported that their work is closely related to what they studied for their degree.

With a job prospect situation this grim for many graduates, it's no surprise that most colleges and other programs put the emphasis on how to get a job. Many students get trained in writing an effective résumé. A smaller number may get

additional preparation, such as learning how to make a good impression in a job interview.

But few students today get any training in how to hold onto that job once they get it. The skills required to succeed in a job may seem to be common sense, but as the French philosopher Voltaire once wrote, "Common sense is not so common." It's no longer good enough to show up for work and "learn the ropes" as you go along. Today's employers need and expect their new hires to start pulling their weight as soon as possible, so that they quickly make a positive contribution to their company.

Internships Are Not Always the Answer

Now some might point out that this is why there are internships. These are low pay (or no pay) opportunities for students to get "real world" experience. In some cases, interns are paired with a caring and skilled mentor who can give advice and help shape the student's attitudes and expectations. All too often, however, the intern is assigned irrelevant tasks with little or no supervision.

I knew one young woman who got her dream internship while she was in college. She wanted to go into writing or publishing, and landed a position with a major publisher in New York City. When I saw her later that year, I asked her how it went. "The most important thing I learned," she said, "was how to look busy." She would grab a stack of folders from her desk, and walk slowly in the direction of the

photocopier room. After spending a little time there, she'd then walk back to her desk again, carrying the same folders. It was better than sitting at her desk looking as though she had nothing to do, which was the case because nobody in the office gave her any work or instruction.

The fact is that too many college graduates are not prepared for the working world. I'm not talking just about academic preparation, though that certainly is a problem for a portion of them. I'm talking about fundamental job skills: what it takes to be a successful employee.

These attitudes and skills can make a world of difference. They certainly can help you be better prepared for the job search process, such as how to make a good impression in a job interview. But they can do much more than that.

Hit the Ground Running

These skills will make you better prepared for that first day on the job and all those days that follow. They will help you make a positive contribution to your company, which in turn will help you keep your job in a time when you don't want to have to start over with a new job search. And by being a better employee, you are likely to get more satisfaction from your work. You will find that the next promotion or added responsibilities come sooner for you than for others who may have been hired at about the same time.

That's what this book is about. Its "secrets" are secret only because few people take the time to tell college students about them. They represent commonsense and practical knowledge that you can use in any job at any level, and that you can use throughout your career.

Unfortunately, you are likely to discover that many of your coworkers don't know these secrets. And what you learn in this book can help set you apart from the rest of the pack.

I expect that you will find these seven success secrets to be valuable to you and make a significant difference in your life beyond the confines of your job. If they work for you, if they make a difference in your life as an employee, please take the time to share them with others, especially younger new hires wherever you may be working. Don't assume that anyone has ever taught them these skills, and make sure that they are equipped to make the most of their time and effort as an employee. They will thank you for it.

Success Secret #1:

Everyone Is a Customer

Congratulations! You have invested years of your time in your college education, and you and your family have probably made a significant financial investment as well. In return, you have gained valuable knowledge and skills that you did not have when you graduated from high school.

This knowledge and these skills will make you better prepared to make a contribution in the working world, and will open the doors to more opportunities than would have been available without your college education.

Lessons from Fast Food

In spite of that investment, I'm going to start in a place that is far removed from the college classroom: your local fast food restaurant.

For many students, a significant part of their work experience comes from jobs in retail settings. In particular, food service is a major training ground for many young people in this country. According to the Bureau of Labor Statistics, more than 3 million people between 16 and 24 years old work in food preparation and serving related occupations in the U.S.; that amounts to 17.5% of all the jobs held by people in this age range. It's likely that a large number of these jobs are in the fast food industry.

In some ways, fast food experience can be valuable training and many of these employees build on what they have learned to become effective leaders in other areas. Sometimes that hard work and attention pays off.

In 1978 at the age of 23, Jan Fields got a job at McDonald's, cooking fries. She rose through the ranks, and today she is President of the company, overseeing an empire of 14,000 restaurants in the U.S.

Obviously, most fast food employees do not advance to executive levels in the company, but that does not mean there are not valuable lessons to learn from the work experience. Too often, however, these workers just see the job as a place to put in time in exchange for near-minimum wages. For many of them, the main goal is simply to make it through the next shift. They don't see the point of trying to seek ways to excel in their job setting.

After all, what can you learn from fast food service that would help you in a corporate job anyway? Most entry-level jobs in big companies bury you in the bowels of the beast, and it is possible that you may never see a customer in your entire career. How can retail experience benefit you in a setting like that?

As it turns out, the lessons learned through fast food and other retail experience can be an excellent foundation for becoming a successful employee in almost any field. It's all a matter of how you look at it.

Here's how this experience can help you succeed.

A Great Place to Work

You may have noticed that magazines and newspapers and other media outlets often publish lists of the "Best Places to Work." People are interested in these rankings because they want to spend their workdays in a pleasant environment. This is not a trivial matter because there are plenty of work settings that are not particularly pleasant places to spend your time.

Television has a way of mirroring reality; we tend to enjoy shows that have elements that we identify with. As a result, sitcoms and dramas often feature conditions that are commonly found in a typical workplace. They may exaggerate them for effect, but we often recognize familiar themes. For

example, there is often a surly or grumpy coworker that makes life unpleasant for others in the office.

In real life, negative behavior can have a real impact on a company. Being grumpy may not seem like a big deal, but consider this. If some people in a work setting don't get along with others, communication among workers is often less effective. If you dread every encounter with a certain person, you may find yourself bracing for a confrontation every time you meet them. If you have to coordinate with this person on a project, or one of you needs the other to get access to information or other resources that are needed to do your jobs, then you are setting yourself up for failure if you cannot communicate effectively with that person.

In the end, you end up wasting time and energy dealing with this negative relationship that could be better spent on doing a better job. And that's not going to help you become a valuable asset to your employer.

This negativity can be even more insidious, however. It might be that you get along fine with all your coworkers, but there are feuds and conflicts between others within the office. This can sap your energy as well. Maybe you just "keep your head down" and try not to get involved. Maybe you have to try to mediate simply to get access to the resources or information you need to complete your work. In short, you end up thinking about these problems when you could be using that time and energy for more productive purposes.

The Cost of Negativity

The problem here is that a negative atmosphere can permeate
the entire workplace. It is no wonder that some employees
might dread coming to work in a place like that. They might
be on the lookout for opportunities to switch to a different
company just to get away from the situation (though there is
no guarantee that the grass will indeed be any greener on the
other side). They certainly won't be nominating their
company for any "Best Place to Work".

Negativity is a real problem. But is it your responsibility to do
something about it? Let's take a moment to analyze the
situation a little deeper.

Who Do You Work For?

So here's a simple question; who do you work for in a job?
As it turns out, the answer may not be as easy to answer as
you might think.

Your quick answer might be "the company" because that's
the name on your paycheck. Or you might think "my boss"
because she is the one with the most power over whether or
not you continue to keep your job.

I'd suggest that both of these answers are wrong, or at least
that they don't go far enough. Think about the question some
more.

One way to answer the question is to follow the money. You get paid with money that the company received from its customers or clients or however it is that it produces revenues. So in one sense, you work for those customers or clients, even though you may never see them.

But if you worked directly for those customers or clients, could you produce the product or service that they are buying, without the help of anyone else? That's highly unlikely. The chances are that they are paying for something complex, and it requires the involvement of lots of people with a variety of skills and experience to deliver the product or service that the customer buys.

So if it were not for your coworkers, your company could not produce the product or service that ultimately pays your salary. In short, you need their participation so that the company can be successful at generating revenue, so that in turn you can get paid.

From this perspective, you work for everyone else in your company. They are counting on you to do your part to contribute, just as you count on them to do their jobs, no matter what level position they may have in the company.

And that's the key to the first secret: everyone in your company is your customer. What can you do to use this understanding to your advantage?

The Customer Experience

Let's go back to the fast food training. Even if you've never experienced it as an employee, you have almost certainly experienced it as a customer. What can you learn from a typical fast food customer experience?

Think about the first thing that happens when you step up to the counter to place your order. In most cases, the person behind the counter says something like, "Hello, welcome to McDonald's. How may I help you?" Does that sound familiar?

It's not an accident that retail employees are all trained to say something like this. They do it because it works; it generates more sales. Let's break it down and see what's going on with this short script.

"Hello." That greeting seems simple enough, but it is really important. It acknowledges the customer's presence. Compare that with an experience you may have had where you stood at a counter for a minute or two before someone came over to help you. Being ignored does not feel good; being acknowledged does.

There's one other part that goes along with the "Hello." Picture someone at a fast food restaurant greeting you. Think about their face. Inevitably, they are smiling when they say "Hello." In order to work, the greeting has to be delivered with a sincere smile. This helps create a friendly, positive

atmosphere for the customer. You get the sense that the person behind the counter is truly glad to see you.

"Welcome to McDonald's." You are being invited in; your presence here is appreciated. Again, it gives you a positive feeling.

"How may I help you?" Compare this with the stereotypical diner waitress who snarls "Whaddya want?" The fast food greeting is an offer of assistance, not a command. It places you at the focus of the conversation, and again is designed to make you feel good.

In order for this greeting script to work, it must be sincere. As you probably have experienced at least once or twice, a bored and tired fast food worker just mouthing the words with a deadpan face just does not make the desired impression.

Note that the employee probably does not know you personally, so this sincerity has to come from someplace other than being glad to see you as a familiar individual. Instead, the retail employee has to have an attitude that the people walking through their door are important, that the success of the restaurant or store depends on the type of experience they have during their visit.

If you can have that attitude, then you can be sincerely glad to see a complete stranger as a valued customer. And that makes all the difference between delivering a wonderful experience

that will make you want to come back, and an unpleasant experience that could lose you as a customer forever.

The Big Question

My question for you is this; why do your coworkers deserve anything less from you than they'd get at the nearest fast food restaurant? If they truly are your customers, don't they deserve to be greeted warmly and sincerely?

Think about how it makes you feel to be welcomed when you arrive somewhere, even if it is a place that you've been to before many times. It probably makes you feel good, and helps create a positive attitude in your mind about being there.

Now think about applying that same strategy to your workplace. If you can greet your coworkers every day with a sincere smile and a friendly hello, it will make them feel more positive about you and their workplace. If you can call them by name, so much the better but it's not absolutely necessary. (I admit that I'm terrible with names and it can take me a while to learn them.) And remember that you *should* be glad to see them, because they are there to help the company make the money that pays your salary.

A friendly greeting for your colleagues—the people you work with—is important. But don't limit this to just the people on your level in the organization chart. You may start at the bottom in your company, but you won't always be there.

No matter what level you are on, remember to apply the same principles to support staff. The receptionist, the cleaning crew, and the workers in the company cafeteria all deserve a sincere, warm greeting from you. After all, you are counting on them to do their jobs so that the company can make money and be a success. You want them to feel good about their workplace, and to look forward to coming to work each day.

And don't forget those above you in the org chart, either. Just because they are your supervisor or manager, or your boss's boss, or head of the department, or even CEO of the company, you're counting on them to do their job well, too. A warm and sincere greeting is always welcome, and you will help them feel more positive about you and their work.

What Goes Around

How much difference can one person really make in a corporate setting? You might be surprised. Think about how just one person with a negative attitude can cast a shadow across a whole group. Then think about how one friendly person can give you a lift, and make you look forward to seeing that person again.

If you find yourself working in a setting surrounded by positive, friendly people, congratulations! It's not unusual, but you should consider yourself lucky to be in such a place and go with the flow.

The fact is that your workplace is more likely to have a less than perfect atmosphere. In a situation like this, you want to be one of the people who try to make it a little better, and not one of the people who make it worse. Sharing some genuine warmth and respect is a great way to help make it better.

You may not see any immediate changes, but stick with the friendly greeting for the people in your workplace. They will be glad to see you, and if you're viewed as someone who is good to have around, you're more likely to be successful in your work. And in the unfortunate event that your company has to downsize, your positive contributions may help keep your name away from the top of the list of potential layoff candidates.

So remember that everyone at your workplace is your customer. You want them to be happy that they have come to work, because you want them to help the company be a success so that it can continue to keep you employed. Develop a warm and sincere greeting to make them feel welcome, so that they know you are glad to see them. It's a little thing to do that just takes a moment, but it can make a world of difference.

Success Secret #1
Action Guide

Think about a time when you felt embarrassed or
disrespected in a store or a restaurant. What are three
elements of the experience that made it so unpleasant?

1. _____

_____

2. _____

_____

3. _____

_____

Think about a time when you received really excellent
customer service in a store or a restaurant. What are three
elements that made this experience special?

1. _____

_____

2. _____

_____

3. _____

_____

Think about three things you can do to give a coworker a good experience when you meet on a daily basis.

1. _____

_____

2. _____

_____

3. _____

_____

Success Secret #2: Make Everyone's Job Easier

Have you ever been part of a group activity? Maybe you have played a team sport. Maybe you have been involved in a performance group, such as dance or music. Maybe you have been part of a group like scouting, or a fraternity or sorority.

Think about when you were working together as a group on a project or activity. Did someone ever do something that made it easier for you to do your part? It might have been something small and seemingly insignificant.

For example, baseball players do a lot of little things for each other. If a runner is left on base at the end of an inning, one of his or her teammates will often bring their hat and glove from the dugout to save them some steps. This practice is known as "picking up" your teammate. Or maybe you know

someone who brought an extra pencil to a rehearsal in case someone else needed one to take notes from the director.

These little acts can turn out to have more significance than you might see at first.

Thoughtful Acts

In order for a person to help in a small way like this, he has to be thinking of someone other than himself. He needs to realize that someone else needs something, and that he is in a position to help. And then he takes action based on that realization.

Whether the beneficiaries of these acts really think about it or not, on some level they are aware that someone else did something helpful for them. And these demonstrations of thoughtfulness and respect make them feel good. So a small helpful act can contribute to a positive atmosphere.

Next, this sort of behavior can be contagious. As with the baseball players, it becomes a social norm to "pick up" your teammate. This can help spread the positive feeling and foster a sense of teamwork, of shared purpose within the group. It is a tangible sign that the individuals respect and value each other.

And this kind of act can help everyone involved do their part better. Saving a few steps for the baseball teammate when it does not take you any more steps conserves energy and saves

time, helping the game move forward. If you can make it easier for a colleague to do their job, it can deliver benefits for them, for the company, and for you.

Visible Dividends

I first understood the power of making someone else's job easier when I was responsible for public relations for a public school district. The school board was dealing with a complex and contentious issue that was getting a lot of attention in the press. I prepared a one-page fact sheet with some of the key statistics involved with the issue, and gave a copy to all the reporters from the area newspapers that came to cover the next school board meeting.

When their articles appeared in the papers, we were happy to see that they had used our numbers, which helped support the board's decision. And the reporters appreciated the fact that I had saved them time by thinking about what they might need in advance of the meeting; they didn't have to follow up after the meeting to request the information. And this made them think more positively about the board and the district administration. This grew into a favorable relationship where the reporters knew that they could count on me for information to help them with future stories.

Taking Care of Typos

Here's another example. In my early days as a freelance writer, I remember talking to a more-experienced writer one

day about proofreading our articles before submitting them
to the editors at the magazine where we both worked.

I said that I wasn't too bothered by the little mistakes I made
because the editors all used word processing programs that
included spell checkers that would catch the errors
automatically. Why should I spend time correcting something
that the editors would be able to fix quickly on their own?

My colleague pointed out that she was very careful to correct
any errors in her drafts before she submitted them. She also
went back and compared the editor's version of an article
against her original draft. This helped her spot mistakes that
she was making, so that she could correct them in future
articles before she gave them to the editor.

I took that advice to heart, and from that day, I worked hard
to improve the quality of the writing that I turned in to the
editors. And something very important happened; the editors
noticed the difference. They soon learned that they had to
spend a lot less time fixing my articles than they did with
articles from other writers.

By saving them time, I made their job easier. They were able
to edit more articles in less time. And they were always happy
when they opened up one of my articles to edit because they
knew that it was going to be less work for them.

Ultimately, this came back to benefit me in some very
tangible ways. When an editor had an article to assign, they

often would choose me over another writer because they
knew that I would turn in "clean copy" that would save them
time and make their work easier.

A Little Thought

Look for opportunities to make your colleagues' work a little
easier. I'm not suggesting that you do their work for them,
especially not if it jeopardizes your ability to get your
assignments done on time. But look for opportunities where
you can save them a little time or effort without having to
take any extra steps on your own.

For example, maybe you need to scan certain publications or
news feeds for information that is relevant to your work. If
you notice an item that might be useful to a colleague, it just
takes a few moments to forward that information to them.
You may have found something that they might otherwise
have missed, and it could help them do their job better.

Or maybe you have to pick up your office mail from a
mailroom. Perhaps you could offer to bring back the mail for
a colleague if you see any waiting there. It doesn't take you
any extra time, and it saves them time. Maybe they will do the
same for you sometime when you are under time pressure.

Note that this does not apply to just the people you work
with directly. There are plenty of opportunities to help out
someone else at work. For example, if you're not on the
cleaning staff, your job description probably does not list

keeping the workplace clean as one of your responsibilities. On the other hand, if you see a piece of trash in the hall, you could take a moment to pick it up and carry it to a wastebasket.

The same holds for keeping your work area tidy; if the cleaning crew comes through and vacuums the floor in the off-hours, you can help them out by making sure that you don't leave items on the floor that would get in the way of them doing their job.

These are little things that do not take much time or effort on your part, but everyone benefits and you've made the cleaning crew's job a little easier (even though they'll never know about it.)

Don't Hand Off Trouble

There's an important corollary to this secret about making someone else's job easier, and that is to avoid making their job harder if you can.

One way that you can make someone's job more difficult is how you deal with problems. In any job, there will be times when you don't know what to do or you can't do what needs to be done. In these cases, you need to get someone else involved who either knows what to do or has the authority to get something done. (Note: just ignoring the problem and hoping that it goes away is almost always the worst choice.)

Let's say that the problem requires additional resources, such as a new purchase or the help from some other department in the company. You may need someone above you in the organization to make that happen. What you don't want to do is go to your manager, and just dump the problem on him. That just makes their job harder.

Instead, along with the problem, offer what you think might be a workable solution. Don't just give your manager a problem, but also give him a way to solve it. This can save him time and make his job easier.

Don't be surprised or upset if your manager does not use your suggested solution. There may be other factors involved that you don't know about that could affect her decision. Perhaps some similar solution has been tried in the past and didn't work. Maybe there are budget limitations, or the department that you think can help is already overloaded with requests for help. And don't be discouraged if your manager doesn't think your solution is a good idea. The important point is to show initiative and that you're mindful of the manager's time, that you want to make her job easier if you can.

Also keep in mind that this works both ways. Don't dump a problem on someone below you in the organization without some suggestion of how to make it work. Maybe you need a large number of copies of a report, but don't have much time. Rather than dump a rush job on the person responsible for

copying, maybe you could ask for a smaller quantity to meet the immediate need (such as planning for a meeting) and get the balance later in time for the actual meeting.

The Golden Rule in Disguise

Here's this success secret in a nutshell: make your coworkers' jobs easier if you can, and don't hand off problems without at least offering a possible solution. In other words, treat them the same way that you would want to be treated. This doesn't mean that there won't be times when your coworkers make your job more difficult or dump problems on you; that's an unavoidable part of any job. But you should do your best to make others' jobs better if you can.

Underneath this motivation, there's an even more fundamental principle in play here. By thinking of what impact your actions might have on your coworkers, your effort to help reduce that impact shows that you have respect for that person's time and workload.

The best way to get respect from others—whether at your level, or above, or below—is to show respect for them. And when you are respected in the workplace, you are more likely to succeed than those who are not.

It's as simple as that.

Success Secret #2
Action Guide

Think about a time when someone did something to make your work easier. Maybe it was a teammate in sports, or maybe it was a family member when you were working on a project together.

    1.   What did they do for you?

_____

_____

    2.   Was this a "big thing" or a "little thing"?

_____

_____

    3.   How did it make you feel?

_____

_____

Which statement describes you best?

❑ I like to do my own work and let others worry about doing theirs.

❑ It makes me feel good to help out someone else when I can.

You just realized that you may have trouble completing an assignment on time in your job. What approach are you most likely to take?

❑ Work harder and hope for the best.

❑ Go to your supervisor, explain the situation, and suggest a possible solution.

❑ Go to your supervisor and say that you can't get the work done in time.

Success Secret #3:
Dress for Success

Of all seven secrets in this book, this is perhaps the one that appears to be the most obvious, but actually has some subtle depths to consider.

Of course, this is an obvious piece of advice. You have to dress appropriately for your workplace environment. Everyone knows that. But have you stopped to think what that's really all about?

Instinctive Behaviors

The psychological principles behind this whole question are really quite interesting. By choosing how you dress for any situation, you are actually trying to tread a fine line between belonging to the tribe and setting yourself apart as an individual.

Consider animal behavior. Members of the same species often have nearly identical coloration. All robins look more or less the same, and their general appearance is quite different and easily distinguished from other birds, such as blue jays. All robins conform to what they instinctively share as the concept of what a robin should look like.

If you look carefully at a bunch of robins, however, you will notice subtle differences in their appearance. Each one has distinct markings that other robins use to tell one individual from another. This is the case with most animals, from insects to fish, from deer to chimpanzees.

There's one interesting aspect of this behavior based on individual and group appearance; it does not pay to be too far out of the norm. A robin with bright, clean plumage will be attractive to potential mates. But if a robin were to have a neon-red breast, it would be too much. It would look strange to the other robins. When an animal's appearance strays too far from the group norm, it may well be shunned by the others. In some cases, the rest of the group can even turn on the strange-looking individual and kill it.

People Are Animals Too

It should not surprise you too much to realize that we are susceptible to the same instinctive behaviors. Think back to your high school experience (though it's possible that your college experience may not be too different). Were there "tribes" whose members could be readily identified by the

way they dressed? These groups often get names such as preps, jocks, goths, freaks, punks, skaters, or nerds, but even if you didn't know what to call them, you could probably tell if an individual belong to one group or another.

In each case, there may have been some distinctive feature common to the tribe, such as a polo shirt or UGG boots worn with shorts or all black outfits or very baggy jeans. These badges identified that person as part of the group.

These visual cues are there to help people identify individuals who share a common purpose or set of values. This is why sports teams wear uniforms. "Uniform" means "the same" and team members wear the same outfits so that they (and the observers) can tell easily who is on the same team.

You also see this in other groups ranging from choirs to volunteer organizations, to security personnel, to medical workers. The clothing makes it quick and easy for an observer to identify an individual as part of a known group.

You stray from these norms at your own risk. You probably can think of at least one person from high school whose appearance was just a little bit "off." Maybe he wore his pants too high or too low, too short or too long, too tight or too loose. And chances are good that people tended to stay away from this person; it may have been difficult for him to make friends, to fit in. It probably wasn't just because of the way that he dressed, but his appearance didn't help matters either.

Context Counts

The key point here is that in any situation involving other people, you need to consider what your appearance signals to others. And while you can use variations to identify you as an individual within the group, if you stray too far from the accepted norms, you risk being viewed as an outsider and being rejected by the group.

As a result, we constantly balance between our desires to belong to a group of some sort, while still trying to retain some traits that will mark us as individuals.

To make matters more difficult, the rules change depending on the situation. For example, few women would wear a formal dress on a trip to the beach, any more than they'd show up for a prom wearing a bikini.

How does this apply to the workplace? First you need to consider the fact that, at the workplace, you share a common purpose with your coworkers. Your jobs are designed to help make the company successful. If the company is successful, it will be able to continue to pay you to do your work, and maybe even give you opportunities in the future to take on new responsibilities that can make that work even more fulfilling.

So when you "dress for work," part of what you're doing is trying to find a way to signal that you share that common purpose with your colleagues. This is an appeal for

acceptance by the group, which can be important for your success in your job. It is also a sign of respect for the others; you show that you accept the norms that the group has established for what they view is "appropriate" dress for the workplace.

Aim High

Here's where it gets a little more complicated. You want to be accepted by your coworkers, so you want to dress in a way that they can identify with you, and see you as being one of them. But I do not recommend that you dress just like them. Instead, I believe that you should dress for the job that you want, not the job you have.

What does this mean and how do you put it into practice?

In most cases, you will start off at an entry level position for your job category. You may be somewhere in the middle of the org chart, or you might be at the very bottom. But in most cases, you will aspire to a better position. Promotions usually come slowly, and in difficult job markets like this current one, they may seem to take forever. But when one comes along, you want to make sure that you're in the best position possible to be considered for it.

One of the best ways to do this is to look the part. This means that you should dress as though you already have the promotion. If your colleagues wear sport shirts with the shirt

tails hanging out, but your department manager wears a collared shirt tucked in, then that's what you should wear.

Remember that people identify with others who dress in a similar way. So when the boss looks around the room and sees you dressed "a cut above" the others, this will register on some level, even unconsciously. It can result in an attitude that you may have "managerial potential" or whatever trait it is that is needed to get the additional responsibilities. And you could end up on a short list of promotion candidates.

Accelerate Your Progress

I remember one particular instance of this strategy resulting in success. As a freelance writer, I wrote for many major magazines, most of which were based in Manhattan. I often had to go into the magazines' offices to do some of my research, and so I got a lot of experience with different companies and their staff.

I recall one specific young man who was hired for an entry level editing position at one of these magazines. None of the other associate editors wore coats or ties. They dressed neatly but "business casual" was definitely the norm. The editors above the associates often wore sports coats, and some wore ties. The Editor in Chief and other senior managers wore suits.

Initially, this one associate editor dressed like the others, but after a few months, he started wearing a suit. In my opinion,

this was a bold move on his part because it jumped over the style of the next level in the organization, and looked more like top management.

But it paid off. Of course, it did not hurt that that this young editor was very good at many aspects of his job and he had talent and skills. He also worked very hard and put in long hours. But his clothes also set him apart from his coworkers, many of whom were also talented and skilled. Within a few years, when some of his fellow associate editors had moved up to the editor position, he was off heading up his own section. And shortly after, he was in charge of the content for a major website.

While I can't credit his success entirely to his suits, I have no doubt that his dressing style set him apart from the rest of the group and helped him gain the attention of his superiors.

But Not Too High

On the other hand, you don't want to stand out too much. My daughter landed an internship one summer during college, and she was thrilled to have a job in a big city. She got dressed up every day, projecting what she thought was the image of a young professional woman.

The problem was that the office was very casual, and she was more dressed up than even the owner of the company. She stood out in an inappropriate way, and after a word from her boss, she toned down her wardrobe so that she fit in better.

If you overdress, you risk appearing over-eager, or at worst, a possible threat to your immediate superiors. So emulate your supervisor or manager, but don't overshoot.

When You Have No Choice

It is unlikely for most jobs, but you may find yourself in a position where you have no choice about what to wear. For example, many healthcare positions require that you wear a specific uniform. Even when it appears that there is no room for personal expression, you can find ways to use how you dress to your advantage.

As an illustration, let's return to the fast food. Even if you've never held one of these jobs, chances are good that you've at least visited such a restaurant where all the staff wears a uniform, such as dark slacks and a company-logo polo shirt. In many cases, managers dress differently—perhaps wearing a coat and tie if they are male—to help make it easier to distinguish them from the line workers. In such a case, there's no way for you to dress like the next step up.

However, how you dress can still make a statement. For example, if you change clothes at work, you can dress for the next level before you work, and then change back to that after your shift. If you're arriving for your shift in a dress shirt and tie, this will set you apart from your coworkers who show up wearing a random t-shirt.

Even when you're in "uniform" in a fast food job, you still have choices that you can make. If you have to provide your own pants in a "slacks and company shirt" setting, then the quality and condition of your pants will make a statement. If they are always clean, fit you well, and are in good condition, that can set you apart from your coworkers who may not take as much care in how they dress. It's amazing how much difference there is between a pair of pants with a crisp crease and a pair with ragged cuffs that drag on the ground.

The next time you're in a fast food restaurant, take a look good at how the staff members are dressed and see if the differences make any impression on you. Who do you think is more conscious about how they appear, and what does that say to you about their attitude about their job? If you had to pick out one or two, who do you think will get promoted next? Does their appearance play a part in why you chose them?

The point is that even when your choice of clothing is limited by your work environment, you still can make choices that will help you stand out and make a better impression on both your coworkers and the managers.

Make a Statement

You don't have to give up being an individual just because you have a job in a company, but if your appearance is too far from expectations, it can hurt your chances of being

successful in that job. Remember that your clothes will speak even when you don't say a word.

If you want to be considered for additional responsibilities (and the rewards that go with them), then make sure that the way you dress says this clearly. Your appearance can say a lot about how much you share the values and goals of others in your company. It can indicate which group within the company you identify most with, and if you're aiming to be a success, then you'll want to be associated with others who are already successful.

Success Secret #3
Action Guide

Think about the clothes you have on right now. Pick three items and explain how they help identify you as part of a group:

1. _____

_____

2. _____

_____

3. _____

_____

Pick three items that you have on right now and explain how they help set you apart as an individual:

1. _____

_____

2. _____

_____

3. _____

_____

Think of three situations where you would dress differently than you are dressed now. What are they, and what would you wear?

1. _____

_____

2. _____

_____

3. _____

_____

Success Secret #4:
Over-Deliver on
Your Promises

Have you ever been shopping, and the salesperson gave you a little something extra with your purchase? Or maybe a waiter or waitress in a restaurant gave you an extra helping with your order? How does that make you feel when something like that happens? In general, it makes people happy to get a little bonus, when their expectations are exceeded.

Delivering more than is expected does not only work in retail settings; it works in the office as well.

A Tale from the Dark Ages

My last salaried position was in the Superintendent's Office of a school district in Connecticut. This was at the time that personal computers were just becoming available (think

Apple II and Radio Shack TRS-80). The Superintendent of
Schools was responsible for putting together the district
budget every year, and it took three secretaries typing and
proof-reading for a full day to put out just one draft version
of the budget, and there would still be lots of typos and math
errors.

I knew about the first spreadsheet program for personal
computers (it was called "VisiCalc") and I got a copy for the
one microcomputer that we had in the office. It took me a
day or so to design the spreadsheet and enter all the data, and
right before lunch one day, I delivered the first computer-
generated budget draft to the superintendent. He was
impressed, but looked at me sadly and said, "I'm really sorry,
but the Finance Committee met this morning, and they
changed a bunch of the maintenance numbers. Can you
possibly have another version ready for me before the School
Board meeting tonight?"

I told him that I'd get it done in time, and took the new
numbers from him. I headed to my office and got to work.

When he came back from lunch, I walked into his office and
handed him a completely updated version of the budget using
all the changed numbers that he had given me. It was all
perfectly printed with no typos or calculation errors. And I
didn't have to pull any secretaries away from their normal
work in order to get it done. Needless to say, he was
favorably impressed.

What Happened Here?

Let's take a look at this story. The key elements were that my boss needed me to complete a critical task and there was a hard deadline for accomplishing it. I was certain that I could meet his deadline, and accepted the assignment. I was confident that I could do the job in much less time than was available, but I didn't promise that I'd get it done faster than his original deadline.

Why didn't I promise delivery after lunch? In the first place, I might have been wrong about how long it would take to make the changes, or I might have run into some unforeseen problem with the computer or the printer. So I put his mind at ease and told him that I'd have the revised report ready in time for the meeting, which was all he cared about at that point.

Then I worked on it right away; I gave the project the top priority that it deserved. And I completed the work in less than an hour (much of which was taken up by printing it on the slow printer that we had at the time).

I was then able to deliver the report well in advance of what I had promised. This made his job easier (see Secret 2) because it was one less item he had to worry about for the meeting that night. And it gave my coworkers plenty of time to make photocopies of it and add it to the packet of other materials for the board members. This meant that I made their job

easier as well, because they didn't have to rush to do that at the last minute.

In the end, my reputation within the office was enhanced simply because I was able to over-deliver on my promise.

Consider the Alternative

Not everyone takes this attitude towards their work, whether it is in their job or in their college assignments. I'm sure you know plenty of people who—at least in some circumstances—do what they consider to be the minimum acceptable for a given task. (I certainly was guilty of this myself in college on more than a few occasions.)

If an assignment calls for 1,000 words on a topic, these people carefully watch the word counter on their word processor tick up until it hits the target, and they're done. Reports get turned in right at the deadline, or maybe even slightly later, but never sooner.

In a work setting, these same people make sure that they take all the break time that their contract allows (and a little more, if nobody seems to care). They hit the door at 5 PM, leaving whatever work that is still undone for the next day. Their work effort is unremarkable, and they tend not to get noticed.

No Need for Super Powers

On the other hand, I'm not advocating that you put in nights and weekends of free overtime on your job (unless, of course,

you work in a setting such as a law office where these sorts of work hours are expected). The key to over-delivery is to take on tasks that you know you can accomplish to the requested specifications, and then do your best to do better than those expectations.

In my case, I was able to complete the task in less than the expected amount of time. You might encounter situations where you are expected to research a subject or provide some analysis of the data. You might be able to dig a little deeper in your research than expected, or provide an extra layer of analysis, and still deliver on time.

For example, suppose your boss asks you to make travel arrangements for an out of town meeting. You could come back with a list of airfares and departure times, which would meet the minimum expectation for the assignment. Or you could find out the time and location of the meeting, figure out the ground transportation options and transit times, and then offer a travel plan that would get your boss to the meeting in plenty of time. You might even offer options that cover public transit, car rental, and cab or limo service, so that your boss could compare the costs and travel times.

Or perhaps it may be as simple an item as formatting your work in a certain way. If your boss has to compile data from a lot of different reports, for example, you might be able to format your data in a way that will save him or her time when it comes to adding your information to the mix.

And I'm not suggesting that you try to over-deliver every time. In some cases it won't be possible to exceed expectations in the time you have available and still get everything else done that you have to do. But eating lunch at your desk on occasion to put some extra polish on an assignment can pay off in the long run.

What Is at Work Here?

When you over-deliver, you send a number of important messages. First, it shows that you can not only do your job, but that you can do it with excellence. When it comes time to think of someone who is in line for additional responsibility, you will be more likely to be on that list.

It also shows that you think beyond just the boundaries of your own job description. You can see how your work fits into a larger puzzle. You want the company to succeed, so you consider how your work affects that of your coworkers as well as your boss, and your boss's boss.

This has a number of benefits. By acting this way, it will help you feel this way. You may be surprised by the personal fulfillment that you can experience by being part of a successful team that not only achieves its goals together but excels at them. If you can do a relatively simple task with excellence, you'll find more satisfaction in your work, especially when you recognize that it's part of a larger effort.

A good friend of mine is now an executive in a snack food company. It's far from what he intended to do when he started out, but he loves his job and it gives him a great deal of satisfaction. "People have so much trouble in their lives," he says. "We're able to give them treats that taste good, that make them smile, that make them feel good. And that makes me feel good."

And when you have this sort of attitude, it gets noticed. Again, it may not be explicitly expressed by your boss and it almost certainly won't result in overnight changes, but in time you'll find that you get picked for better projects and get special assignments where your contributions will make a difference.

So don't expect a trophy when you over-deliver on an assignment. Your boss may not even acknowledge that you exceeded expectations—keep in mind that bosses have plenty of alligators in their own swamps to cope with—but every instance will be one step toward your continued success. And you will become a more valuable employee, which means that you will be more likely to keep your job in the event of down-sizing, and more likely to be chosen for new responsibilities and advancement.

Success Secret #4
Action Guide

Think of a time when you did more than was expected of you. It might have been on a class assignment, or a school project, or in a sports setting. What three things did you learn about yourself from this experience?

1. _____

_____

2. _____

_____

3. _____

_____

Think of three ways that you can complete a task so that you deliver more than was expected:

1. _____

_____

2. _____

_____

3. _____

_____

Which statement do you think describes you best?

❑ I do what I have to in order to get by.

❑ I like to do what is expected of me, no more and no less.

❑ I feel good when I complete a task with excellence.

Success Secret #5: Communicate Early and Often

One of the great skills of humans as a species is our ability to accumulate knowledge. Isaac Newton once wrote in a letter that "If I have seen further, it is by standing on the shoulders of giants." In other words, his great contributions to math and science were only made possible by building on the work of others who had gone before.

Why do I bring this up? It is because knowledge is worth nothing if it cannot be communicated. If you cannot take what you have learned and share that information with someone else so that they can benefit from your experience, then that learning benefits nobody but you.

In fact, I would argue that while the primary goal of education is to help you learn from the discoveries and

experiences of others, an equally important goal is to give you the skills to communicate clearly and effectively. Whether it is in writing, or using the spoken word, or by some other method, you must be able to communicate what you know if it is to be of any value. That is why hiring managers often list communication skills as the Number One general skill that they look for in a job candidate.

If you choose not to communicate—or are not able to communicate effectively—in your job, you can create serious trouble for yourself because you reduce your value to the company.

The Box in the Driveway

Let me share a simple example of why communication is so important. We recently ordered something online and had the box shipped to us by one of the major package delivery services. Now, this particular service has had an excellent track record with us and our regular driver is conscientious and efficient. Unfortunately, that driver was on vacation and the company put a substitute driver on our route.

We live in a suburban area, but in an older home that is set way back from the road on an interior lot. As a result, our driveway is more than 200 yards long, and you can't see our home from the street. To complicate matters even further, there are two buildings on either side of our property at the street, and they share our driveway for the first 30 feet or so before splitting off to each side.

The delivery service has a communications link to their delivery vans, and instructions will come up when the driver gets a given address. In our case, the instructions read something like "Leave packages by first door on driveway."

This substitute driver got to our driveway, saw that it split in three directions, and was confused. Which building was the one with the door by the driveway?

I want you to stop reading right here for a moment and think about what you would do in this driver's place. What would your next move be?

Do you have your answer ready? Here's what he actually did.

The driver took the box, left it where the driveway split in three, and recorded it as having been delivered "to the front door." We were lucky that the box was still there when I discovered it later, since it was in sight of both the street and a fairly busy public bike path. Anyone could have walked off with the package and it is unlikely that anyone would have noticed. And I'd never have known that the box had been "delivered" so I'd have no idea that it was missing.

Communication Choices

What could the driver have done differently that would have been a better solution? The answer is that just about anything would have been better. Leaving it at the door of either of the adjacent buildings would have been an improvement. Even

taking it back to the depot and saying he was not able to deliver it would have worked.

Best of all would have been if the driver simply called the dispatcher and confessed that it was not clear which was the right building. Maybe the dispatcher could provide him with more information, or could call me for more instructions.

Instead, the driver chose not to communicate about his confusion. Perhaps he did not want to get behind schedule, or he wanted to avoid embarrassment, or he didn't want to look like he couldn't do the job.

By not communicating right away, however, the driver ended up creating trouble for himself as well as for the company and the customer.

The bottom line here is that your communication skills are as big an asset as your knowledge, and you must remember to use them. Problems do not go away if you simply ignore them, and in some cases, they can fester and grow into much more serious situations. And people will often remember what went wrong for a lot longer than they will remember what went right.

The flip-side of the secret about over-delivering is that you also need to be able to deal with situations when things do not go according to plan. And when they don't, you should be prepared to let someone know about it.

When Bad Things Happen to Good Plans

Let's face it; there will be many times when you won't be able to complete a task with the level of excellence that you might want. Sometimes stuff happens that you just can't predict. If you break your leg and wind up in the hospital, it will probably take you longer to get a given assignment done and you might miss your deadline.

Or maybe there's a malfunction in your computer, or the network, or the printer, or the copy machine. Or perhaps you need information from somebody else in order to complete your task, and they are late getting it to you, or it's incomplete, or there's something else wrong with it that either delays your work or slows you down.

It can also be as simple as getting conflicting instructions. For example, you might be told that you have to produce a certain report by Friday, without fail. And then your supervisor hands you a rush assignment that needs "top priority." If this new job puts that weekly report at risk, which do you do first? Should you just go ahead with one or the other and hope that you've made the right choice?

Some of these factors may be predictable, and some may be under your control, but in many cases they are neither. So what do you do?

Let's get back to basic principles. As an employee of the company, you are part of a team. It is in your best interest for

the company to be successful. Part of that success comes from dealing with problems and solving them before they become bigger problems. So you should want to help resolve troubles when you can.

Take the Long View

The key is to communicate about problems early, rather than wait to see if they will take care of themselves (which they rarely do). This also means that you need to plan ahead and take responsibility for a long range view of your work.

For example, be aware of how you spend your time at work. Are you working efficiently? Are there parts of your "routine" that don't make good use of your time? If a crunch situation arises, what are the first things that you could skip that would not impact on getting your assignments done?

Also, plan ahead. If you know that you have a major project due in a week or a month, be aware of how much time you'll need to spend on it each day or each week in order to get it done on time. If something unexpected crops up, you need to know right way whether or not it threatens your ability to complete your other tasks when they are due.

You want to communicate about problems as early as possible, but you can't see trouble coming if you're not looking out for it.

No matter when you realize that there is a problem, however, you need to tell someone. How do you go about doing this?

Pick the Right Person

Perhaps the most important step is to bring the problem to the attention of the right person. When in doubt, you should talk to your immediate supervisor. There is a chain of command in any organization, and while it may seem arbitrary and even an obstacle to getting work accomplished at times, it exists for a good reason.

An organization's structure is based on the idea of shared responsibility. It works best when specific people are in control of part of the operation, so that they can make decisions and implement them in order to get tasks accomplished.

In return for your paycheck, you make your time and skills available to the company. Your immediate supervisor is responsible to make sure that those resources are used to best advantage to advance the company's goals. It may not always seem as though the company is making the best use of your resources, but the management will have other factors to consider besides what you think.

At the same time, your supervisor is also responsible for protecting you from demands from other parts of the company that might prevent you from completing your assigned work. So when you encounter a problem, your

supervisor is the most likely person that you should communicate with about it. As discussed in "Make Everyone's Job Easier," you should try to offer a possible solution when you bring a problem to your supervisor's attention, though there may be other factors involved that you don't know about that might make your suggestion not a viable solution.

It is also true that there may be times where your supervisor might be part of the problem, or where there are some other factors that might make you hesitate to communicate through normal channels. In these rare occasions, it can make sense to get advice from a coworker that you trust and who has experience in dealing successfully within the company. This person may be able to provide additional perspective on the situation, and have ideas for the best way to approach your supervisor. Or this person may be able to suggest an alternative way to communicate the problem to someone who can deal with it effectively.

One point in this process is crucial; you want to avoid making anyone in particular look bad, if at all possible. Even when the situation is the result of some individual's action (or inaction), blame is rarely a productive component of a successful solution. And even if a certain person's lack of ability or other deficiency is a major cause of the problem, the chances are good that your supervisor is already aware of it.

So focus on the specifics of the problem and what it might take to fix it, and leave the blame game alone.

Take Action Early

Remember the fable of the little Dutch boy who found a leak in the dike. If left alone, the leak would have grown until the dike failed and the land would be flooded. He took action right away to plug the leak and prevented the small problem from becoming a much larger one.

Or consider an ocean-going freighter. These heavy ships can require miles to stop or turn around. If an obstacle is identified early enough, a small course correction can be made to easily avoid the problem without any loss of speed toward the destination. If the obstacle is not spotted until the last moment, however, it will take a lot of energy and emergency action to avoid a collision. And if the collision cannot be avoided, it can result in a costly disaster.

So it is with problems in the workplace. Fix the ones you can on your own, and be able to identify the ones that you can't fix by yourself. And if it's a problem that you can't fix and that jeopardizes your ability to get your work done or threatens an important project or function, bring it to someone's attention early. It is not always easy to do, but it is likely to prevent the problem from growing into an even larger one.

Going back to the example given earlier in this chapter, what do you do when you have two assignments that conflict? If you wait until one or the other task is due but still incomplete, you've run out the clock and left your supervisor with no way to get the job done in time. Instead, if you can bring the conflict to someone's attention early enough, the solution may be as simple as a revised instruction; "Get your weekly report completed as early as you can, and then get this new task done as quickly as possible." Or your supervisor may be able to put someone else on one of the tasks to help you get both completed on time.

Communication is a key skill, but it is made much more powerful when you also use it in a timely fashion. A message is valuable, but only when there is enough time to act on it.

Success Secret #5
Action Guide

Imagine that you have been asked to call a friend's mother and give her an important message because your friend is tied up in a meeting and can't be interrupted to make the call himself. When you call the number you were given, it turns out to be disconnected. What would you do next?

_____

_____

_____

_____

_____

_____

Think of a time when you put off dealing with a problem. Maybe you waited hours or days or even weeks to face it. Think about how that felt, and how the situation turned out. What are three reasons why it would have been better to deal with the problem sooner?

1. _____

_____

2. _____

_____

3. _____

_____

You have been working with a professor on one of her
research projects, and you have discovered that a large
portion of the data may be missing. What are three things you
can do to present the problem in a way that is most helpful
and productive?

1. _____

_____

2. _____

_____

3. _____

_____

Success Secret #6:

Be Flexible

A classic feature of Zen Buddhism is to draw instruction from nature's examples. One of the best-known is the lesson that can be learned from bamboo. This plant grows fast and tall, and you might conclude that it is fragile. To the contrary, a stalk of bamboo can absorb great stress from wind or other forces. It bends with the force but does not break, and then when the stress is removed, it bounces back straight and tall again.

Plenty of Stress

When you start your first job, there are plenty of opportunities for stress in the workplace. Depending on the situation, you may have many coworkers with whom you must interact on a daily (or hourly, or even minute-to-minute) basis in order to get your work done. As with any given group of people, it's not likely that you'll be drawn to become best

friends forever with all of them. You may not find anyone that you would count as a close friend. Yet you'll need to get along with all of them. And getting along with a group of individuals can be stressful.

In addition, you'll have one or more people who are responsible for supervising you, assigning you tasks, and evaluating your performance. Their assessment of your work will count for a lot more than just a grade at the end of a semester; it will determine whether you continue to have a job with that company and the regular paycheck that goes with it. In other words, making a living depends on what they think. And that can be stressful, even if you get along great with them. (Again, it is quite possible that you won't get along great with all the people in the supervisory or management positions above you.)

Those are just the interpersonal sources for stress. Then there's your work. You may receive contradictory instructions, such as being told that two different tasks are your top priority. Or you may find yourself pressed just to get a single task completed in time. Or you may find yourself having to deal with a coworker who is uncooperative or unpleasant. Or it is quite possible that much (or all) of your time is taken up with simple, repetitive tasks that may not challenge you as much as you'd like. The absence of challenge can be as much a source of stress as too much challenge can be.

Be the Bamboo

Learn to reduce stress by bending with it. Don't fight the force that is weighing on you, but instead find ways to let it flow past you and leave you still standing. This often requires that you be like the bamboo and bend with the stress so that you can bounce back when it is relieved.

Now it's one thing to make a cool reference to Zen philosophy, but it's a whole different matter to put that philosophy within the gray-walled confines of a corporate cube farm. So here are some practical examples of ways that you can bend in the workplace.

Let's start with a common situation. You are tasked with a job that is repetitive and it does not seem to make good use of your skills. The job needs to be done, however, and for now the company expects you to be the one to do it, so we'll start by accepting that. In any group activity, there will be times when an individual's talents may not be used to their fullest. (To be honest, the same holds for solo practitioners such as me; much of my days are filled with tasks that have nothing to do with my particular skill set and experience, but it's just part of doing business.)

Also remember that those "trivial" and mindless tasks are stepping stones to success. You won't get big responsibilities in your job until you have proven that you can deliver on the small ones.

So what can you do? Some people choose to whine about how much they hate the work to anyone within earshot: coworkers, supervisors, even outsiders. That is hardly a way to promote a positive working environment, and definitely does not reflect well on you as an individual. Some others simply hold it in, and let the anger and frustration fester inside. Don't think that this won't show on the outside in your facial expressions, your body language, and even your speech. That strategy is only slightly better than the whining approach.

There's a third way to consider. Do the job, but if it requires less than your total effort, then figure out something else that you can do that is productive while you work. No, checking Facebook does not count as something productive. Remember that being part of a company means that you have a shared purpose. When you're working for the company, your efforts should go toward advancing the company's goals in one way or another. With a little creativity, you might be able to augment your boring, repetitive work with something else that can add value to the time you're spending.

Nobody Home?

When I was in college, I had a part time job for a while where I made phone calls for a telephone survey company. A dozen of us worked in the evening in a small office lined with telephones. We had a written script that we had to follow word-for-word, and we would be given a column of names

from the phonebook that we would have to call until we completed a survey, then we'd get another column of names. This was in the days before voice mail, and the people often were not home when we called. So we'd just let the phone ring and ring until we decided that weren't going to pick up, and we'd move on to the next number.

Needless to say, listening to phone numbers ringing endlessly was pretty mind-numbing. I chose to make something out of this "wasted" time. I started to chart how many rings it took before someone answered the phone. I'd let it ring ten times before I finally hung up. After about a week of charting this data, I discovered that the chances of anyone answering after the sixth ring were about zero. I took this data and my analysis to my supervisor. After he studied it, he issued new instructions to all the callers: "If nobody answers after six rings, hang up and try the next number."

Instead of surrendering to the boredom, I added an extra task of my own to my work. It did not require any additional time on my part; I still made just as many calls per hour as I had before I got the idea to track the number of rings. My extra research did not cost the company anything extra. And I got lucky. I managed to make a discovery that showed a way to save the company money. By knowing that it was best to hang up after six rings instead of hanging on for ten rings, the callers spent 40% less time on calls that weren't answered. As a result, they were able to make significantly more calls per hour. And that meant that it cost the company less for each completed survey. And I helped the company be more successful.

Matchmaker

More recently, I had a company as a client for a few years that had to process a lot of data each month. The data came from a variety of sources, and it had to be put into a consolidated spreadsheet.

Part of the problem was that the different data sources used different model and part numbers to refer to the same product. The people working with this data had to figure out what the correct model number was so that it would be recorded correctly in a large database for analysis. They developed "cheat sheets" that listed the products for a given data source and matched them with the correct model number. It would take hours to go through some of the reports to clean up the input data. If they made a mistake in matching or missed one, it would produce an error in the database and they'd have to go back and try to find where they made the mistake and then enter a correction.

I worked out a way to use a feature called "lookup tables" and macros in Microsoft Office Excel to automate the matching process. Once you had paired a part number from a given data source with the correct model number, the process would automatically match them in the next month's report. I managed to reduce the amount of time required to process this data by several hours per report, and improved accuracy

at the same time. As a result, the company had better data faster, which helped save them time and money.

When you're stuck doing something repetitive or mindless, be on the lookout for ways to use the talents and skills that your company wanted when they hired you in the first place. You may be able to identify a way to do the job better or more efficiently, or you may be able to find new ways to get more information out of the data you already have. Keep in mind that your "improvements" or other discoveries might not always be adopted or even appreciated, but it's still better to look for ways to make an additional contribution than try to just get by with the minimum.

Impossible Deadlines

One of my favorite sayings is "This project is so messed up that not even Wilbur and Orville could get it off the ground." There are times when circumstances will conspire and in spite of the best efforts of everyone involved, the wheels fall off. How can you deal with this sort of stressful situation?

The first step is to be as prepared as you possibly can be. When I'm driving, I try to always be aware of my best "out" in case something goes wrong. If the car ahead of me blows a tire or swerves to avoid a hazard, I hope to have left myself with enough space to react and find a safe place to get out of the way.

You need to do the same with your work, if you can. When you have an assignment, don't pace yourself so that you complete it right at the last moment. If possible, aim to get it done early. You can use the extra time to get caught up on other projects, or to put a final polish on this one. But it leaves you with a little slack in which to deal with the unexpected: the network crashes, the printer breaks, or the copy machine is down for service. If you have not painted yourself into a corner, you'll have more flexibility to deal with the unexpected when it arises. And you'll be less stressed.

It also leaves you with more room to maneuver if some new assignment crops up unexpectedly. My daughter's first job after college was working for a small company run by a pair of brothers. From time to time, some crisis would develop and one of the partners would come running out of his office yelling, "It's time for everyone to stop what they're doing and save my life!" Histrionics aside, this is a perfect example how some new task can appear suddenly. If you're already ahead of schedule on your own work, then you'll be in a better place to pitch in when something else goes wrong.

There will be times when there is no perfect solution. This is where communicating early becomes so important, as does being flexible. If you have to stay late in order to get an unexpected task completed on time, be prepared to do so. No, you don't want this to become routine (unless that's already part of your work environment's culture, such as

some legal practices), but there are times when it is unavoidable.

So if you're able to be flexible, roll up your sleeves, and pitch in without complaint, that's a contribution that is likely to be noticed. Don't expect extra compensation (unless you're in an hourly wage position which may require that you receive overtime pay) or extra time off in return for the occasional extra hours. If you get one or the other that's great, but it's also important to help work for the success of the company.

Take Note

One of the most stressful times at any job is when you are just starting out. Everything is new and strange, and you have so much to learn. Most businesses are facing serious financial constraints, and they need new workers to become productive as quickly as possible.

As a result, you're likely to get hit with a barrage of new information when you start your new job, and this can create a lot of stress all by itself.

This problem is not limited to new jobs, however. It also occurs whenever you start a new project or assignment. There can be lots of specific details to remember about what needs to be done, and how, and by what deadline.

If you miss some of these details, it can negatively affect the quality of your work. If you are constantly going back to your

supervisor to check on the details or to get the instructions
repeated, you are wasting both her time and yours.

One simple solution to eliminate this stress is to carry a small
notebook with you at all times. When you get any
instructions, write them down. This will help you keep track
of all the details without having to stress about whether or
not you have remembered them correctly.

This is a trick that I learned from taking flying lessons.
Airplane pilots are in constant communication with Air
Traffic Control, and the information that is exchanged can be
of critical importance. I'm talking about life-and-death here.

Most pilots keep a notepad strapped to one leg so that
whenever they are given an instruction by Air Traffic Control,
they can write it down right away so that they don't forget it.
And this system has another important feature; when the
pilot gets an instruction, she then repeats it back to the
controller. The controller then either says "Readback correct"
or repeats the information if the pilot got it wrong.

Learn to do the same thing with your instructions. If your
boss tells you to call a customer and gives you the phone
number, write the number down in your notebook and then
read the number back to your boss. This will make sure that
you have written it down correctly, and you won't have to
come back to your boss to check on it later. And your boss
will know that you care about getting the details right, and he

will have one less thing to worry about. (Remember that bosses have stress of their own.)

Habits such as carrying a notebook with you can go a long way to help reducing stress on the job.

Interpersonal Stress

Sometimes it's not the work that stresses you, but the people you work with. You don't have to be best friends with all your coworkers. You don't even have to like them all, and frankly, it's unreasonable to expect that you would if the group is large enough. You do have to get along with them even though that can be difficult at times. The ability to work well with everyone and earn their respect is a key leadership attribute, so keep this in mind if you want to be thought of as a candidate for additional responsibilities.

Sometimes the solution can be as simple as being flexible in your schedule. Perhaps there is one person who you find difficult to be with at work. Perhaps they are outspoken with their negative opinions about work or other coworkers. Perhaps they are vocal about political or religious views that run counter to your own. Lunchroom discussions can be stressful under these conditions, even if you're just listening and not participating in the exchange. The solution might be to simply time your lunch break differently (if that's an option). Getting there just 15 minutes sooner or later than this difficult person can make a world of difference in your attitude and stress level.

Or perhaps you have a coworker who likes to drop by for a "visit" while you're working, and makes endless small talk. You don't want to be rude, but you may need to concentrate in order to get your work completed. Be flexible and think about what might be behind the visitor's behavior. Maybe they need a sympathetic ear; perhaps you could arrange another time during the day when you would have time to chat. (If you can arrange to do this either at their workspace or in neutral territory such as a break room, it will make it easier for you to end the session and go back to your work.) Or perhaps they don't have enough to do and are just bored. Consider asking them for advice about how to complete your tasks; this might make them aware of how much you have to do.

Don't Take It Personally

Another important way to control stress at the workplace is to keep your emotions in check. When someone critiques your work or finds fault, especially if that someone is your boss, it's easy to take it personally. You can over-react, get defensive or angry, or maybe just burst into tears. Doing this does not help anyone, especially you.

If you're work is not up to expectations, learn from the criticism and do better the next time. This is not a personal attack on you; it is simply an evaluation of the work that you did. Getting emotional about negative feedback does not help

the situation, and is not going to enhance your reputation in
the workplace.

Also, don't rise to the bait if a colleague "loses it." Keep in
mind that they are responding to their own stresses at work
and in their personal life. If they get angry or emotional, even
if you feel that it is directed at you, don't respond in kind.
Relax, respond calmly if you can, or just walk away if you
can't.

Just remember to take a deep breath and move on.

Learn to Bend

The key to all these situations is that you need to be flexible
so that you can bend with the situation. Try to understand the
forces at work, and then find a way to bend with them so that
you can still get your work done without having to stress over
relationships with coworkers or tight deadlines or boring
assignments.

Success Secret #6
Action Guide

Which statement describes you best?

❑ I hate boring work. It makes me crazy.

❑ I enjoy finding the challenge in any assignment, whether it's easy or difficult.

❑ I can turn my mind off when I have to do repetitive tasks.

How does stress affect you personally? Do you worry a lot? Do you try to make accommodations for the unexpected? Are you able to just ignore problems and not let them bother you?

_____

_____

_____

_____

_____

Think of three things that you can do to help you bend with
the forces that stress you.

1. _____

_____

2. _____

_____

3. _____

_____

Success Secret #7:
Always Be Marketing

Here's the biggest secret of all. I don't care what your job description says or what your boss says your work responsibilities are, here is the Number One Priority for you in your job, no matter what position you hold:

You are responsible for the success of your company.

Now, you are not responsible for it all by yourself (unless you're a solo practitioner, like me.) In most jobs, you have coworkers, and they too are responsible for the success of your company. But if you don't share in that responsibility, why should they bother giving you a paycheck?

How can you act on this understanding? One way is to do your job well, as has already been mentioned here. Work hard, help solve problems rather than create them, show initiative, respect all your coworkers at all levels and do what

you can to make their work easier, and everything else that we've covered to this point.

But it goes beyond that. Way beyond.

Someone Is Listening

Whenever people meet someone new, there is a short list of small-talk topics that make up just about every initial conversation. Here they are:

- Where you are from

- What school you go to (or went to)

- Your family

- The weather

- Sports

- What you do for a living

There is a reason that people like these small-talk topics so much. They are more or less fact-based, as opposed to topics like religion or politics which get into issues of values and opinions, and thus are open to disagreements. Getting into an argument is not a great way to meet someone new, so people tend to stick with the fact-based topics.

This also gives them an opportunity to seek connections, to find out ways that you are similar or have shared interests. People naturally tend to try to find ways that we are like each other, rather than how we differ, so these questions provide relatively safe ground for exploration.

For people out of school, it's almost inevitable that the conversation will sooner or later get to the "What do you do for a living?" question. (It's about as inevitable as the "What's your major?" question for those still in college.) And how you reply can make a big difference. Here's an example.

Hot Summers

I love ice cream, but I've never worked in an ice cream store. The fact that I love ice cream is part of the reason that I've never worked in a store that sells it because I might eat too much of it. Another key reason, however, is a conversation I had with someone I met when I was in college.

He worked in an ice cream store in the summers, and told me that they got to eat ice cream for free. That sounded great to me, but then he told me that after a few days, people got tired of ice cream and stopped eating it even though it was free.

I figured that I would rather keep my love of ice cream intact rather than risk losing it by getting a job in an ice cream store, so I never considered working for one. That one person's comments kept me from a line of work, and who knows what

contributions I might have made to the store—or even the whole chain—had I started to work for one.

I have not mentioned the name of the chain that this person worked for, and with good reason. In the same conversation, he explained to me how he and the other workers used to cool off in the summer when business was slow. I won't go into details, but let me just say that he seemed to think it was thoughtful of them that they took their shoes and socks off first.

Now, I realize that this probably didn't happen all the time in that store, and maybe it never happened in any other stores in that chain, but I still have that image in my mind. And when I want ice cream, I choose to take my business to a store from any chain but that one.

This one casual conversation with a person has colored my view of that company for decades. At the time, I doubt that either of us had any idea that his remarks would have such a lasting impact.

What Will You Say?

When someone asks you what you do for a living, what will you say? What will you say about the company you work for, and about your coworkers?

It's easy to complain about your working environment. It's always easier to throw bricks than bouquets. I've never heard

of a single job that didn't have some aspect that was not particularly appealing. Whether it's the workload, or the type of work, or that one particular coworker who drives you crazy, it's understandable that you would want to unload some of that. You might think that having a conversation with someone who isn't involved might seem to be the perfect opportunity. And you would be completely wrong.

The fact is that you rarely know who you're talking to in a conversation like this. Your audience is often much larger than just that one other person. Who will they repeat this conversation to, and what will they say?

Think of Facebook for a moment. You might post a comment on your wall for your contacts to see, or you might comment on someone else's status update. Who can see what you wrote? The audience for your remarks almost always extends far beyond just your Facebook contacts. If someone else comments on the original status post, then all of their contacts can see the whole thread of comments, too. And if any comment in the thread draws attention, it's possible that thousands of people will be able to read what you wrote.

Another reason to be mindful of what you say about your work is that the other person is trying to find connections with you. Those connections can be either negative or positive. Think for a minute about the conversation I had with the guy who worked in the ice cream store. I like ice cream, so when he mentioned where he worked, that stuck

with me as a connection. And when he went on to say some
negative things, those comments registered with me. To this
day, I can't remember his name or even where we met, but I
do remember the negative things he told me about his job
and his company.

Don't Say It

Remember the old saying: "If you don't have something good
to say, don't say anything." This is good advice when it comes
to talking about your job away from the workplace. While it's
one thing to sort through the dirty laundry with your
coworkers on the job in order to try to make a situation
better, it's another thing entirely to share that sort of negative
information with someone outside the job. This even applies
to conversations with friends and family; you can't be sure
whether or not they might repeat what you say to someone
else.

On the one hand, there's the chance that your remarks could
find their way back to someone in the company who might
take exception to what you said. In the worst case, it might
cost you your job, but that's unlikely. It still could damage
your reputation at work, and put a hold on your plans for
advancement and increased responsibility.

Even if your remarks don't get back to someone at work,
however, it's still likely that what you say could reach
someone who might do business with your company. That
friend or neighbor or new acquaintance may not be involved

directly as a customer or supplier, but you don't know everything about their family and their friends and their neighbors. Maybe one of those connections is an existing customer or client, and hearing bad news about your company might affect their decision to continue to do business with it. Or maybe your comments will reach someone in the banking or investment industry, and color their opinion about the fiscal health of your company.

It's Also about You

Keep in mind that your negative comments about your company or coworkers can also reflect badly on you as an individual. If people view you as someone who whines or complains, that could affect their opinion of you; who likes to be around someone who is negative?

Even worse, people might get the idea that you are not loyal or that you lack integrity. Loyalty, integrity, and ethics are values that employers rate highly. If you get a reputation for being deficient in these areas, it can damage your opportunities not just within your company, but if you should look for a new job in another company, that reputation could follow you there.

The person that you say these things to are part of your personal network. That network is one of your prime assets in making connections for your work and for finding job opportunities. You don't want to do anything that might make people in your network hesitate to recommend you to

someone else. Your personal network is probably your greatest asset when it comes to finding a new job, so you don't want to damage that resource.

Keep in mind that this is also holds true for posts that you might make online to your network of friends, such as on Facebook. You may feel like posting "Hooray! It's Friday and I can't wait to get out of this hell hole and get a drink. Or three!" but think about what this says about you and your attitude about work. There's no way to un-ring that bell once you post something like that.

Help Your Company

Fortunately, this powerful word-of-mouth effect works both ways. Take pride in your company and what it does, and this will show through when you talk about your job. Every company has its problems, but they also have strengths. Learn to talk about what your company does well.

You don't have to make a sales pitch to every person you meet, but why not leave them with a positive impression about the company and its products or services? It probably won't make any difference, but there's always that chance that you'll be talking to someone who is connected to someone else who could bring a lot of business to your company.

It's possible that your name might even be connected to this increase in business. "My wife met your employee, Jane, and heard about your product which might be just what we

need." Even if you don't have a sales position, being mentioned like this is the type of positive influence that supervisors and managers notice, and it can be a boost to your reputation.

Even if the gains are not attributed to you in any way, even if you don't know that there is any connection at all to what you said, the increased business still comes back to benefit you. If the company is more successful, it is less likely to lay off workers. It is more likely to be able to continue to pay your salary. And it is more likely to grow, resulting in the creation of new positions within the company, which means increased opportunities for you to advance and get new responsibilities. What is good for the company is almost always good for you.

It's also possible that someone you speak with will be impressed by your attitude, and it might result in a job offer or other opportunity somewhere down the road. Just as negative remarks can follow you for a long time, positive remarks can enhance your reputation long after you have a conversation.

So why would you want to say anything but positive things about your company when you talk about your work? In order to do this well, you'll want to make sure that you understand your business so that you can talk intelligently about it. You should know about your company's strengths; what does it do better than its competition? You should know this in any case, so that you have a more strategic

understanding of your company and what you and your coworkers are trying to accomplish.

If you can talk for a minute or two about the positive aspects of the products or services, you may find that you can plant seeds that can grow success for your company, and directly or indirectly, for you as well.

Success Secret #7
Action Guide

Think about a time when a friend or family member said
something negative to you about an experience they had with
a store or restaurant or even another person. How did that
affect your opinion of that store or restaurant or person?

_____

_____

_____

_____

_____

What is your Number One responsibility in a job, no matter
what your job description might say? What can you do to
meet that responsibility?

_____

_____

_____

_____

_____

Which statement describes you best?

- ❑ I need to say what's on my mind, and I don't care who I say it to.

- ❑ I keep my thoughts to myself.

- ❑ I feel good when I can recommend a good resource to someone.

Put the Seven Secrets
to Work for Your Success!

As I said from the very start, these "secrets" are commonsense principles that anyone and everyone can apply to their work. They are only secrets because few people take the time to share them with new workers.

They all boil down to one simple idea; if you bring a positive attitude to everything you do in your work and your personal life, you are more likely to be successful. Treat people the way that you want to be treated: with respect and appreciation. It doesn't matter if they are your friends or your coworkers, your bosses or support staff.

Everything else follows logically from that simple, basic idea.

Let me bring this back to the quotation I listed at the start of this book:

Watch your **thoughts**,
  for they become **words**.

Watch your **words**,
  for they become **actions**.

Watch your **actions**,
  for they become **habits**.

Watch your **habits**,
  for they become **character**.

Watch your **character**,
  for it becomes **your destiny**.

From your thoughts to your future, there is a natural connection. You cannot control or predict your future, but do what you can to increase your chances for success and happiness, no matter how it is that you measure success for yourself.

If you make the effort to think positive thoughts, the rest can follow naturally. Your thoughts will shape your words, and in turn your actions. In time, those actions will become habits, which will help define how other people see you. And if they tend to see you in a positive light, this can affect your destiny and help bring you success.

I'm not saying that this is easy to do. Any setting—but especially the workplace—can have influences that make it difficult to maintain a positive attitude. You need to work at

focusing on what is good in your setting, not because of some vague notion that the universe will reward it, but rather because there are solid reasons based on psychology and other research that shows exactly why this approach can work in your favor.

I hope that you will find ways to put this information to use, and that it will help bring you security in your job, satisfaction in your work, and success in your pursuit of advancement. And if you find that the points made in this book have helped you, please don't keep them secret. Take the time to share these insights with others, so that they too can be happier and more successful in their work too. That will only add to your success.

Put the Success Secrets to Work
Action Guide

At this point, I'd like you to spend some time with the illustration that you've seen at the start of every chapter in this book. Here it is, one last time:

Pick out one of the silhouetted characters in the image above, and just based on what you see, make up a story about that person and their views about their job and their workplace. What do you think their attitude might be?

_____

_____

_____

_____

_____

Based on the information covered in this book, imagine that
this person is your friend. What are some of the questions
you might ask them—or some of the things you might tell
them—if you wanted to help them become more successful
in their work?

_____

_____

_____

_____

_____

Now I'd like you to pick another character from the image,
and go through the same process. Make up a story about their
situation. How is it different from the first person that you
chose? What can you say about the second person's attitude?

_____

_____

_____

_____

_____

And once more, think about what you'd like to tell this
person to help them become more successful, to find more

satisfaction in their job, and to reach their goals of more
responsibility and professional success faster. What would
you say to them?

_____

_____

_____

_____

_____

About the Author

Alfred Poor, PhD, is an accomplished speaker and writer. He has written or co-authored more than a dozen books, and thousands of his articles, reviews, and commentary have been published in major magazines including Business Week and PC Magazine, and online for FOX News, Verizon, and Hewlett Packard, among others.

He has been the keynote speaker at a range of events, including the Trenton Computer Festival (where he was preceded by Bill Gates of Microsoft and David House of Intel the two years before he spoke) and the Evolution Magazine Small Business and Technology Boot Camp. Some of his speaking and training clients include:

- Marsh & McLennan

- The Hartford Insurance Group

- CIGNA

- The Video Electronics Standards Association

- Wesleyan University

- Temple University

Alfred is known as a speaker who uses humor and energy to deliver concepts that his audiences can put to use right away. Here are some comments from audiences and meeting planners:

> "Alfred is a wonderful speaker with rich and diverse experience."
> *Joseph Facchiano, JoFash Enterprises, LLC*

> "I have had the pleasure to hear Alfred Poor speak. He delivers his content in a very easy to understand format. For me he made the complicated seem simple. Anyone attending will take away techniques that they can implement immediately."
> *Ken Varilek, Elite Human Solutions Inc.*

> "Alfred Poor energized the audience with his dynamic presentation and mastery of his subject. Many participants sought me out to say how much they enjoyed his talk and how they gained information that they could put to work now. I am already planning to include Alfred in some of our future events."
> *Darnell Davis, Evolution Magazine*

> "Alfred Poor was just what we were looking for—an experienced speaker who was very familiar with the key factors that are moving our industry. To me, the most amazing thing about Alfred was how he handled

questions. Perhaps you have experienced people who can go on for what seems like an endless interval asking an obtuse and convoluted question that many cannot comprehend. Invariably Alfred restated these questions for the audience, phrased better than each of the questioners could have conceived. What a skill! It was a delight to have Alfred speak to our chapter. We would invite him again in a heartbeat."
Joel Pollack, Director, Bay Area Chapter of the Society for Information Display

For more information about Alfred Poor and his services, you can find out more at his website at *www.alfredpoor.com*. You can also contact him by email at **alfred@alfredpoor.com** or by phone at **215-453-9312**.

Follow Alfred on Twitter at @AlfredPoor.

Alfred has a career skills presentation designed specifically for college audiences. This program is ideal for seniors, in the fall to energize them for their final year, or in the spring to help launch them into the working world. It is also ideal for Career Week or Career Fair programs, or as an adjunct to résumé and job interview training programs.

Alfred will help promote your event, and offers discounts for block bookings when he can schedule additional engagements in your area at the same time. He is the easiest and most professional speaker you will ever work with.

For a brochure about this program or to schedule a presentation, send an email to **college@alfredpoor.com** or call **215-453-9312**.

Alfred Poor is a member of the National Association of Colleges and Employers (NACE).

www.ingramcontent.com/pod-product-compliance
Lightning Source LLC
Chambersburg PA
CBHW021241090426
42740CB00006B/643